WOMEN WHO ^{still} LOVE
CATS too MUCH

WOMEN WHO still LOVE CATS too MUCH

By Allia Zobel Nolan

Cartoons by Nicole Hollander

**Library of Congress Cataloging-in-Publication Data
is available through the Library of Congress**

© 2015 Allia Zobel Nolan

ISBN-13: 978-07573-1872-6 (Paperback)
ISBN-10: 07573-1872-X (Paperback)
ISBN-13: 978-07573-1873-3 (ePub)
ISBN-10: 07573-1873-8 (ePub)

Publisher: Health Communications, Inc.
          3201 S.W. 15th Street
          Deerfield Beach, FL 33442–8190

Text copyright ©2014 Allia Zobel Nolan. Visit www.AlliaWrites.com
Illustrations copyright ©2014 Nicole Hollander. Visit www.NicoleHollander.com
Book design by Tom Greensfelder

For God; my grandfather, Louis Frank; my husband,
Desmond Finbarr Nolan, who *still* puts up with my obsession
with the puddies; together with my two fur balls, Sineady Cat, the Fraidy
Cat, and Nolan Nolan, as well as women everywhere who are hooked on
a feline.

—A.Z.N.

Toots! This book's for you, my one and only . . .
because you wouldn't have it any other way.

—N.H.

For all the cats who've made me what I am today:
a covered-in-hair, cat-codependant, broke, "kneedy" woman who
loves her cats (and every other fur ball she comes within inches of)
way too much ... if that's possible. My thanks to Oscar Pookie,
Scruffy, Vanessa Dahling, Winston Stanley, III, MacDuff, the Bold, and
Angela Dah-ling.

Introduction

I admit it. I'm a woman who *still* loves cats too much.

It's an addiction I've had from birth and one I've struggled with all my life. Okay, but things have changed since I initially wrote the first edition of this book. I've become more mature. I understand the dynamics of my obsession better. I've made more concerted efforts to course correct.

NOT!

Okay, so I'm still putty in my puddies' hands. But over the years, I *have* managed to cut back ... a bit ... a tiny bit ... a little bit. ...

Truthfully, I haven't cut back at all. How could I with those soulful eyes boring holes right through me? Look, there are worse things. I could eat bags of flour. Or be a hoarder.

Besides, cats are more popular now than ever before. So people are more understanding. Once they've been head-butted by their own itty bitty little fur baby, I'm sure any notion of skimping would be impossible. I mean, I don't know for certain, but I can guess Grumpy Cat's mommy has designer kitty litter flown in from France—the way I do for my darlings. And can you imagine a star like GC dining on anything but the finest sushi and $25-a-slice imported ham?

I'm afraid some might say I still put my cats before my husband. But hey, he's gotten used to it.

With two felines in my bed, (two of which are 20 and 23 pounds, respectively) a filtered waterfall that emits a grinding noise like a dysfunctional garbage disposal and plays havoc with my bladder, Kibbles in the drawer for midnight feedings, the door ajar with a heavy leaded cat statue so they can go in and out at leisure, and two step ladders perched so the babies have easier access to the bed, hubby has decided a room of his own wouldn't be such a bad idea. I mean, it's not as if I kicked him out or anything.

As for my friends, most of them couldn't put up with my codependency. So they're long gone. However, my true-blue buddies, though they may not understand my addiction, take me as is, covered in cat hair and smelling of Feliway and fish. They understand if I'm not always available and, on the odd day that I am, that I'll have to Skype the puddies every 15 minutes, and always, always take home two kitty bags of gifts as an offering for my absence.

Of course, my kitties each have an iPad to play with. And their own iPhone to text mommy in emergencies when, for instance, they need someone to scratch them under the chin or pad into the living room to get their favorite catnip mousie.

But I know those are poor substitutes. What my darlings really want is Mommy . . . at home 24/7 . . . adoring them face to face and catering to their every whim. I used to step out for the mail each day. But the meows were so loud and so soulful that I finally had to hire someone to do it for me.

Still, it's not as if I didn't try to seek help. I went to a twelve-step program. But the only thing I got out of it was what I gleaned from the others: things like what stores sell fresh-squeezed organic tuna juice, and recommendations for kitty massage therapists.

So you might say, I'm still a work-in-progress. I know I shouldn't be so wrapped up in my cats that I forget to have a life myself. But then, what kind of life would I have if I couldn't do all I can for my four-legged progeny?

Then too, I realize with the recent upsurge in adoration of cats that a lot . . . I mean a lot . . . more women (and okay men, too) are probably struggling with the same problems I have.

That's why I am reprising and adding up-to-date info to this book—so all you cat addicts can have the benefit of my experience. (Did you hear a meow?) So you'll know you're not alone. So you'll realize there are probably thousands, even millions of us out there who love our cats too much. (I'm sure I heard a meow.) I want you to know that even though I can't, you might be able to—with resolve, perseverance, and time—assert yourself and learn to put your family, friends, and yourself first, and the cats second.

But honestly, would you want to? (Now that definitely was a meow. Gotta go.)

—Allia Zobel Nolan

You know you're spoiling your cat (but you don't care) when ...

You buy a ginormous tank and stock it with exotic species so the puddies have a choice when they're craving fresh fish.

You hire a personal trainer to exercise the
cats' arms and legs while they nap
so they don't have to expend the energy.

You know your cat gets the best of everything,
but you wouldn't have it any
other way when ...

You purchase fine bone china cups
and arrange them on the table so puddy can
push them off, at will, onto the floor.

You throw away fifteen or more catnip toys
until you find the one your cat prefers.

You pass up the kitty litter that's on sale
for the designer brand.

You know your cat is taking advantage of you, but you wish he'd do it more when . . .

He gets hot paraffin manicures daily.

He hires limos to take him across the street
to his friend's house.

He has his own no-limit charge account
at Petco and Cats R Us.

You know your cat is manipulating you more than usual when...

She complains because she can't find *Kitty Boo-Boo* on TV, so you switch to another, more expensive cable provider.

She brings you a dead mouse in the middle of the night and you feel compelled to get up and say "What a good kitty," then take a photo for her Facebook page.

He sighs and you immediately run to the cabinet for treats.

She yawns and you hire an architect to build her a kitty activity gym.

You know you're still guilty from that mishap with puddy's tail when...

You buy her a couch to claw but have to return it for a new one because the pattern is wrong.

You buy six robot vacuums so puddy can invite her friends over to play "bumper cars."

You drain your 401k for kitty's matching diamond collar, ankle bracelet, and pinky ring.

You know you might be a tad extravagant
when it comes to your cat
(but hey, what is money for anyway?)
when ...

Your cat has her own iPhone, iPad, Google Glass,
and high-speed Internet connection ... and you don't.

Your dinner consists of discount peanut butter
and peas while the babies eat from specialty menus
prepared by Rachel Ray and Bobby Flay.

You order Tiffany jewelry regularly so kitty
can play with the little blue boxes.

You know you'd go to any lengths to please your puddy when ...

You won't turn over during the night
no matter how uncomfortable you are because
you might disturb the cats.

You hire a high-priced detective to locate your cat's birth father.

You stand in line for six hours to get her an autographed copy of *Grumpy Cat*.

You know your cats are wreaking havoc
with your love life when ...

They make all your dates take a "CAT"
(Cat Affinity Test) to see if they're acceptable.

You can't enjoy sex if the kitty litter needs cleaning.

You know your obsession with your cat is coming between you and your man when ...

During intimate moments you rub your boyfriend under the chin and say, "Nice Kitty."

You go ballistic when your date sits in your cat's favorite chair.

You won't wear the red dress your man loves because the cats prefer you in a cheetah print.

You realize you might be spending a bit too much time with the cats when . . .

You make a rustling noise with the treat bag,
pat the couch four times, and say,
"Come sit by Mommy, precious"
when your new love interest walks in the room.

You gather fur from your cats' brushes
to make earrings.

Your significant other insists you're kissing the cats
more than you're kissing him.

You know your cat is ruining your social life (not to mention your social media life) when . . .

You unfriend anyone who won't "like" your puddies' Catnip Connoisseurs Facebook page.

You talk to your lover in the garage so your cats won't get jealous.

You take your kitty's side when he demolishes
the flowers your sweetheart bought.

You know you suffer more separation anxiety than your cats do when...

You feel guilty if you have a quiet, romantic evening out without your cat.

You install cat flaps in your bathrooms
so kitty can join you when you use the facilities.

You quit your high-paying job at a top
IT corporation because your boss wouldn't
give your puddies a corner office.

You know you're putty in your puddy's hands
(but you don't care) when . . .

You let your cat walk back and forth over your face
without so much as a "pardon me."

Your cat expects you to stand at attention opening
and closing doors for her at her whim.

She jumps up on the table and helps herself
to food on your plate.

You know your cat thinks your primary purpose in life is to (what else?) serve him when . . .

He brings friends home without calling
and expects you to cook.

You set a timer, stop what you're doing, and pet your puddy for 20 minutes every half-hour, despite the fact that you have carpal tunnel syndrome.

You "furminate" your cat, brush his hair into countless options saying . . . "How does the itty-bitty-kitty like this hairstyle?" until he approves.

You know your cat senses (and he'd be right)
that he can do anything he pleases when ...

He unravels your designer sweaters
so he can play with the yarn.

He hops on the dining room table,
sits in the middle of the food, and grooms
himself when you have guests.

He switches programs you're watching
to ones he prefers.

You know you're being too lenient with your fur child but can't help yourself when . . .

She makes a mess and assumes you'll
clean up after her.

You comfort her and say ... "No worries, pet, Mommy knows you tried," when she "misses" the litter box.

You allow her to chew on your toothbrush because she enjoys it and ... well ... just because.

You know your cat is hazardous to your health (but really, her happiness comes first) when . . .

You strain your eyes because your cat is sitting on your glasses and you haven't the heart to move her.

You slip on the dead birds your cat leaves on the stairs.

You get hives when you have to take your
cat to the vet for shots.

You know you worry too much about not doing enough with your cats when ...

You feel obliged to nap with your cats during the day—
then can't sleep at night.

They expect you to make videos of
their midnight crazy antics and get up
at 5:00 a.m. to post them to their blogs.

They insist you order and watch webinars of
"How to Stare at, Squish, and Paint with Spiders"
and "Zen and the Dead Rat" with them.

You know your cats are adversely affecting
your work habits when . . .

You stop in the middle of a presentation,
lick your hand, then rub your face in a circular
motion like your cat does when he's grooming.

You carry your work around the office in
your mouth, meowing plaintively, until someone
pays attention to you.

You ask your client if you can have some of his blackened tuna for your cat.

You know your cats may be putting a chink in your career when . . .

You get complaints from coworkers with allergies about the cat hair on your suit.

Your assistant has a hissy fit when he has to pick up a birthday cake for the cats on his lunch hour.

You get passed over for a promotion because you test positive for catnip.

You realize your cat obsession is annoying others at work when ...

You find your Secret Santa gift
(a designer T-shirt embossed with a photo of
the kitties) in the lunchroom garbage.

No one wants to be your partner at
team-building conferences.

Your boss blows a gasket when you call in sick
because your cat won't play Swat-the-Mousie.

You know your preoccupation with your cats is beginning to cost you friends when . . .

Your BFF refuses to be seen with you unless you stop wearing "tacky cat jewelry."

Your cats insist you wear perfume
made from pheromones and the smell makes
people avoid you at choir practice.

Your kitties hypnotize friends so that
they forget what they came for when they gather
for your cat-addiction intervention.

You know your cats are holding you back from having a good time (but it's a small price to pay for their love) when ...

You win two tickets for a weekend in Venice but give them away because the cats pull a face.

You can never do anything spur of the moment because the fur balls require two weeks' notice when you leave the house.

You feel guilty for weeks after taking a business trip.

You know your cat is lowering your self-esteem when . . .

You crop yourself out of photos of you and your cat because you feel you spoil them.

You blame yourself if your cat sniffs his food, then tries to bury it.

You constantly ask your kitty why a handsome boy like him would stay with such an undeserving woman like yourself.

You know you need to
(but find it excruciatingly difficult to)
stop pandering to the puddies when ...

You ask their permission for some
free time to shave your legs.

You watch YouTube videos of other cute kitties
at work so your babies won't get jealous.

You change your outfit if your cat
looks at you askance.

You know you've become a complete worrywart when it comes to the cats when . . .

You buy your puddy an expensive treat every time you go to the store because you're afraid he might leave you.

You turn up the heat, get out the vaporizer, and call the visiting vet if your cat sneezes.

You feel rejected when your cat sits on the floor
instead of the pillows you just fluffed.

You know your cat is making you a
nervous wreck when ...

You cause a scene in the grocery when
they're out of Fancy Feast.

You cut the handles off visitors' pocketbooks
because you're afraid your cat might get
his neck caught in them.

You pace the floor, popping tranquilizers, when your cat goes out with his friends and forgets to text.

You know you're overprotective
(is there such a thing?)
when it comes to your cats because ...

You give your cat your taser and pepper spray
when he goes out at night.

You call 911 when your cat won't eat his treats.

You insist your vet be checked for fleas
before you take the babies in for a checkup.

You know your cats are throwing
your home's feng shui off
(but you're helpless to stop it) when ...

Squirrel and mice heads are tacked up helter-skelter
on the walls with no thought to your spiritual aura.

Dozens of plain brown paper bags litter your
family room and disrupt your color scheme.

Your furniture is piled up on one side of the room so
the kitties can have a better view of the bird feeder.

You know your cat codependency
can sometimes be dangerous
(but hey, life is a risk) when . . .

You wind up in the emergency room several times
a month so you can get some much-needed
shut-eye—without offending the puddies.

You close your eyes when you have to give the
cat insulin and wind up stabbing yourself.

You test the cats' Kibbles for too much salt and get salmonella from a recalled bag.

You know your cat has you well trained when . . .

You wake up in a panic at the slightest touch of your cat's tiny padded paw.

You spend the bulk of your day
(oh, okay, all your day) making sure the fur balls have
everything their little itty-bitty hearts desire.

You wear their rabies shot disks on a
necklace you never take off.

You know there's no limit to what you would do for the puddies when . . .

You style your hair in the garage because your cat doesn't like the sound of the hair dryer.

You hire an orthopedic surgeon to trim their nails.

You buy them matching outfits and order one for yourself.

You miss the end of your favorite movie because you don't have the heart to shoo your cat from in front of the TV.

You know all it takes is one look from your beloved puddy to make you . . .

Cancel your once-a-month exercise class so you can stay at home and rub her tummy.

Spend your bonus on a compound that makes her thyroid pill taste like caviar.

Let her use up (and offer her more) tissue so she can continue playing "Spin the Toilet Roll" in your bathroom.

You know your overwhelming love for your
puddy makes you do weird things like . . .

Learn how to type with one hand so the
other is free to massage your kitty.

Install video monitors all over the house,
so you'll be able to run and tell your cat how much
you love her the minute she wakes from napping.

Cut your phone calls short because
your cat needs attention.

You know you absolutely positively still love your cats way too much (but can't, and wouldn't dream of changing) when ...

You let your cat lick the salt off your potato chips.

You invite your cats to "kneed" your legs despite the pain.

I could go on. But we're off to the Cat Café for tuna and chai. Okay, so I'm hopeless. Still I wouldn't have it any other way. Would you?

The End . . .

About the Author

Allia Zobel Nolan is the author of close to 200 titles for adults, children, and fur children, including *Cat Confessions: A Kitty Come Clean Tell-All Book; Purr More, Hiss Less: Heavenly Lessons I Learned from My Cat; Whatever: Livin' the True, Noble, Totally Excellent Life;* and *The Worrywart's Prayer Book*, among others. She lives, writes, and loves her puddies way too much in Connecticut, oh yes, with her husband. Visit: *www.AlliaWrites.com*

About the Illustrator

Nicole Hollander's blog Badgirlchats.com can be found online six days a week. A Sylvia archival comic strip appears every day as well as links to politics, cultural commentary, and of course, more cat videos than you can shake a stick at! Visit: *www.NicoleHollander.com*

11/15